NO ONE IS DADDY

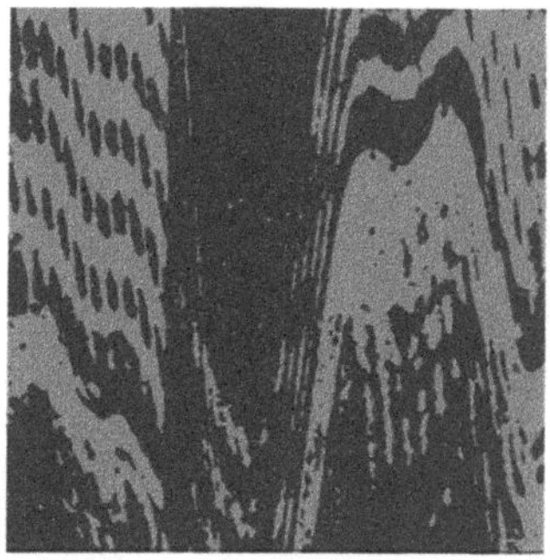

DYLAN KRIEGER

saturnalia | BOOKS

Distributed by Independent Publishers Group
Chicago

Saturnalia Books
2816 North Kent Rd.
Broomall, PA 19008
info@saturnaliabooks.com

ISBN: 978-1-947817-94-4 (print), 978-1-947817-95-1 (ebook)
Library of Congress Control Number: 2025950626

Book design by Robin Vuchnich
Cover image by Christopher Payne

Distributed by:
Independent Publishing Group
814 N. Franklin St.
Chicago, IL 60610
800-888-4741

CONTENTS

EMPLOYEE OF THE YEAR THE WORLD ENDS

the origins of things 5
hustler's gambit 7
whatever it's all for 8
midlife maggot 10
retirement underwater 11
safety in distance 12
permanent zero 15
monsters like me 16
millennial reign 17
undateable 18
common sense 20
soft anarchy 21
terraforming silence 22
ode to the father of my abortion 23
the last fool ever suffered 24
remember the empire 26
one-star review of human nature 28
caption america 29
bathroom graffiti summary of youth 31
futurism in reverse 32
woe to the alpha and omega 33

FULL SERPENT

once worshipped 39
hymn to exes 40
the hierophant hosts a dinner party 42
the red room where no one ever gets what they want 43
the joke 44
playing with plague 45
songs i know 46
crystal disc 47
belief in evil 48
hallowed be the whores 49
all money is drug money 50
very whatever 51
my mother informs me everyone has horses 52

citizens of what 53
gap in the static 55
beta haze 56
the world drain 57
vetting the ether 58
liminal brothel 59
minutia trenches 60
give up like you mean it 61
erotics of the soapbox 62
the art of fact 63
the black box records our defanging 65

NO ONE IS DADDY

vcr's last words 69
fossil of desire 70
hail mary, no one is daddy 71
yes all censors 72
the fallacy of daddy 73
history talking to itself 74
the canker veil 75
lay-off lilies 76
what can perish 77
exhibitionist's nocturne 79
the former order 80
epoch the likes of which 81
print out my insides 82
between commercials 84
textbook anomaly 86
tongue-tied telos 88
cities i won't live in 89
let evil in 90
dawn's dropped jaw 91
loves under construction 92
searchlight 93
disarmed to death 94
the solipsist reaches out 95
impossible gods 96

Acknowledgments 98
Author Bio 99

“‘There have always been” “such men,’ he said” “‘They must be natural…”
“inevitable” … “Am I not this too?” “Or,” “for that matter,”
“am I not you too?” “What would be” “left of you?”

“If you killed me?’”

—Alice Notley, *The Descent of Alette*

EMPLOYEE OF THE YEAR THE WORLD ENDS

the origins of things

at first, there were no spiders to spit on
the rocks just stood there, all naked and baking
the egg came first, but the chicken
cannibalized it out of the historical record
then the wheel learned to weaponize snow
and suddenly even water needed a lawyer
when gods fell quiet, daddy hurried
to fill the silence with commercials
the past was marked down to mere pennies
for a limited time only, memorizing short numbers was necessary
we ordered every major stigma by the designer, in every color
we watched a chain reaction snap in several independent threads
this is my strongly worded letter to the origins of things
daddy long sentencing phase, daddy longer limousine
daddy landlord, daddy debt collector
daddy indented for the reader's convenience
daddy mastermind of modern medicine and non-stick cookware and crusades
pick me up on transatlantic shoulders
drop me wherever the war is today
forget my sins after three hail marys

forgive me when i die too soon
without your blessing, i find myself
grabbing the hands of other tall men at the supermarket
without your pardon from this shitty city
i am just another oracular orphan of stolen fortune
with my tongue against the sunroof, almost free

hustler's gambit

in a stalemate, the only legal move is back into the box
competition without winner, all your try-hard advances called off

i melted the earth's small intestine into a necklace to sell on etsy
i diamond-encrusted my disability for mass consumption at market

on the way from the office to the warehouse to the porn shoot
no smoky footfall pattycakes the floodgates into submission whatsoever

i am ineffectual at barricading the rain, and it says so right here on my résumé
under the section in which i profess love for all companies, conglomerates

and their offspring, under the section in which the gods speak through me
in social security numerology, under the section in which i earned degrees

inside a soda bottle you left sticky and surrendered to a colony of bees
under the section in which i was once smart enough to learn chess

from a dead man and kick his ass, under the section in which i cheated
just by staying alive long enough to rewrite the stalemate

and who cares? all the witnesses have since moved into dark boxes
i wouldn't take them out now, except to estimate their worth at auction

i wouldn't bring up the past except to sell myself hand over fist
portfolio of misremembrance diversified across carefully cropped countryside

i stand before pastoral backdrops, sobbing like the death is fresh
reciting prices of subscriptions—there is no better time to grift

whatever it's all for

i was waiting by the phone back when there were phones to wait by
i was speaking fluent music you were into at the time
i kept the tracking number for the big box of meaning with everything in it
i followed the cute mailman, failing daily to explain the shortage

nothing is ever really lost, except at the sorting facility in itasca, illinois
where i peer out from behind the counter, covered in customs forms
awaiting the executioner, who is still on vacation
awaiting the full-blown package of nonchalant stuffing

today is tied so tight with twine i can't measure its dimensions
only boomers hand out business cards anymore, so i keep mine
at the bottom of the cistern in my parents' backyard
in the belly of first beasts and all their state-of-the-art radar

i personally assure your destruction, whatever it's all for
i'll be ready, at the door, backpack brimming
gorgeous with anticipation—hate me as if love letters
depended on it, as if the love letter were yours

written from a deathbed, by someone you remember
only faintly, from a former life, and it says you were *the one*
yes, who ran away to join the suburban circus, yes
but you've forgotten who this person is

no one in charge ever said it would end like this
but it did: the busy signal, resultless search
unclickable return button smashed into grayscale soup
history is a series of URLs that proves patience is not our strong suit

and i don't know what is, but i know whatever it's all for
is lost on a delivery truck somewhere in the middle of the country right now
and i want to whisper in its soggy, corrugated ear
after nightfall, with no clothes on, just wait there, i'll come to you

midlife maggot

i stayed larval as long as possible
no mother could make a microphone of me

i kept six legs soaking in liquid preservatives
creepshow carefully tied off like a water balloon

i swelled to climax at the curl of your antennae
toward the end of the world, burst before warned

i emerged blank mucus, screeching with feedback
too electrified to touch. the broadcast began automatically

speakers too steeped in the skull to be distinguished
womb voice blasting backward, echo of the egg's first scolding

i stayed larval as long as possible
but mother needed a new microphone

with quick assembly, future-proof, hands-free
she clicked her sticky wings together and out shot solid shibboleth

plugged cleanly into the machine, fuming old buzzwords
i don't even believe, startling every seedpod in earshot

the generation of bad babies, broken open
for the soup inside, ends with me

retirement underwater

after i retire, i'll find midnight and unfold it until all the loose buttons fall out
i'll pry back the past lives of mice from steel traps, light my cigarette
on a terrorist attack, i'll scatter the ashes of newly minted money
from a hot air balloon over the atlantic and a rare breed of sea beast
will breach the surface to eat it, i will pretend that i can swim
so fast the beaches can't keep up with me, that my remote position
mid-ocean is the only reason you can't see me

except in dreams we blame on bad weed, photos our phones
slideshow automatically on the anniversary of any memory
i'd like to retire from the reminder that the pig's head once spoke
back to me and now it won't, that the joke i still tell over drinks
is one you wrote off the cuff on some road trip we don't discuss
i'll sip frozen liquor from a halved grenade with my tits out
after i retire, dream over, too-hot sun dropped in spilled milk

no use crying underwater, but i'll do it anyway, with no oxygen tank
i'll dive down into the surf and come back cured of feelings, singing strange
chipped shells everywhere echoing my choke-ups in their tails
i will turn into the pig's head and speak back to myself
in no language you would understand, i'll tell your joke in new
tongues until i don't recognize you in it, and then i'll retire
even that, i'll look up at long last to no land on the horizon

i'll spread my chapped lips like an atlas and it will be my turn to laugh

safety in distance

ivy league screaming raised me
by the unbeknownst throat
to elephant the vendetta, screwdrive the keyhole
muscle the old world into unpossessed pearls

tenderness ends by definition
in the pit of some pocket
i forgot existed
in the value of a dollar lit on fire

i'm fine with the thunderless wondering
who painted all the windows shut for me
to penknife into cobwebs
desiccated decades later

someone thought, "there is safety
in distance" and then invented me
like a novelty flavor of whipped cream
on the tongue of an advertiser, glowing ultraviolet

oops, i looked back and turned into a pillar of microplastics
i hope i go to heaven before i die and nowhere after
i hope the kingdom of god is buried
facing a different direction than cardinal

and everything we confessed
is reduced to one of those wired-together
heart-shaped structures made of flowers
they put up on street corners where bike accidents happened

i could make one myself
with dandelions and a coat hanger
and place it somewhere no one cares about
like the middle of my living room, or the yukon

i recognize myself in that milky stuff
that comes out of a dandelion stem when it's angry
surprise party for the taste of a gun
i blow out my candles like a teasing little snitch

wishes flinch when i walk by
like they can't fathom why i came
we don't talk about the time
i kicked the heart into new shapes

we don't whisper bare minimums
in the shadow of the crushed funeral sculpture
at golden hour, we don't hold up matching
alcohols and make them kiss

we don't do any of this, because
the heart is made up
i haven't constructed it yet
but when i do, it will be monstrous

the world will claymation for miles around
i'll get the license plates of all my enemies
crash the market, blackmail the government
i'll build the monument just to destroy it

like the rightful parent of last days
with my headache full of unwatched boiling water
in the middle of my living room, or the yukon
one finger in the air like i can tell a better ending

than the elements casually recombining
across microscopic distances in the interstices
of our bodies, where we will reincarnate as
more dandelions, or as a media frenzy, or not at all

permanent zero

at the center of the bloodshot bullseye / i still find you sprawled out / almost by accident / like how the plows back home sometimes / caught condoms full of snowmelt / no one pulled out / we climbed inseminated everests / at every pileup in town / winter gritted us between its teeth / with its pants down
i couldn't stand it / long enough to grow a soul / so i stayed zero years old
smallest target, only practice / for pricking myself out of existence / at the mutant moment / the news is all cried out / commercials brutalize the last song you played / in the middle of the maze / unreal numbers poured from every orifice / no one was afraid yet / about the rower of the bone boat / we figured we would pay / with someone else's sideways eights / we would exchange the out-of-place colossal / for some new playing card / any shape but circle / any timeout but the present / with its ragged paw print / engineering new people / not out of nothing / but from the same old threads / we combed and braided over and over / into astonishments we have no use for now
except to find each other / almost by accident / deep in the plow's mouth
bobbing obscene

monsters like me

some children blow whole nightlights hiding from monsters like me
midwest goodbyes start early so you can hear the end before you're dead
a decades-long tornado siren, special Lord of the Flies edition of Monopoly
in which i am the pig's head, and then a single dollar bill stolen over and over again
and then the surface of reality burns the game into its scrotum
and that's how economies are created, baby: by the loose scabs
dangling from our bodies, more sick fruit, watchful vultures waving hi
from the top floor, the skyline looks like a staticky tv, obscured tapeworm
what if demolition is best witnessed from no distance whatsoever?
no more dilemma of the spectator, just snowfalls of sheetrock
they'd find me curled up under the rubble of your bedroom closet
where no one in their right mind ever believed you that i lived

millennial reign

i slept in on 9/11. Y2K killed my cat. i am the dispossessed crunchy millennial trash all the bar graphs in time magazine warned you about, complete with art professors name-dropping famous rapists, a legal pot leaf drawn into my latte, the eyeballs of venomous spiders winking from my piercings. attempts to film the future frown at me. graveyards watch where they step, for fear of trampling the living. my parents can't remember my america, as if their VCR jammed on a D.A.R.E. commercial and nothing else has happened since, as if the past freezes shut with screaming people still inside it. after the first crash, i made a protest sign with colored markers. after the second, i sucked dick for money. after the popup apocalypse diagnoses my bullshit personality perfectly, i will reach enough enlightenment to step foot on the roof of an airport and not get arrested, and that will be the climax of my movie: standing still and getting away with it.

undateable

in the archaeological record of modernity
the only icons with halos are window blinds

through which streetlights fight to enter
a human eye. i once dated someone

who hung blackout curtains over the insides
of everything. i once dated someone whom i

begged to cut my thigh and drink the blood.
i once dated myself, on a dare, and i hated it

every second in the house no wolf dare blow down
all those bygone years neatly preserved

historicity of criticism of the authentic
provenanced future fodder of scholars

toilet seats and equestrian figurines
survival of the fittest knicknacks ever

dated and dumped and dreamt about
decades later, until the sun wakes death up

i took the blackout down after he left
i don't regret it, except during seasons

or when the landlord peers in too early for
underwear, another halogen desecrated by a face

common sense

today my teeth hurt in a way bones aren't supposed to
the news says i might have a disorder doctors haven't heard of
a deer huffs its uneven measuring sticks
into an orthodontist's parking lot

on my way to work, the thunder quits mid-clap
all the animals startle except us
cocooned by highway, undeterred by weather's
misplaced power strips overflowing with old cords

i get where i'm going with little effort
everyone is an asshole but me
i park my car by the fence just to be by myself
climbing vines into civilized primetime

my makeup melts into my crow's feet
my high heels wobble on loose gravel
another stray balloon from a car dealership
escapes our atmosphere like no one's watching

i pick up several satellites from my computer but none has wifi
my mouth is still obsessed with becoming dust
by lunch, i'm eating heat stroke on the smoke break picnic bench
the balloon and i make eye contact; the rest is just common sense

soft anarchy

one time my friend electrocuted his own dick just by pissing on the wrong surface
sometimes it's like that: freak accident amped to happen at the edge of yet

the salesman in me died a little more tonight, the way the highway trailed off
open parenthesis, pastime personage turned toothless, subtropic tyranny of fleas

feeding my own blood back to me whenever i swallow accidentally
i met the devil the way most kids meet barney or the easter bunny

cartoon cosplay, someone else's party, i wasn't invited
to participate in this soft anarchy but i did anyway, replaced my face

with screeching locusts and a cactus flower, if i were famous
it would be for following the water cycle until it drowns

me out, but by then, you won't be able to hear me
and i won't be able to tell

terraforming silence

on any landline, after the dial tone stops screaming
silence fills with sister, with glacier, with scripture
coated in teflon, lead, asbestos, from the rotary basement extension
to the second story, we held unwitting animals up to the receiver
hissed back at their voices through the ventilation system
i wanted to talk to someone other than myself, at lost last
across ridiculous distance, scraping the edges of time zones
against thumbsucker-style crooked teeth, yell-singing
the national anthem before strat-o-matic baseball tournaments
over takeout, through the answering machine, inside several walls
the old words rattle, like raccoons still live in the attic
we hear the stomping of insects we exterminated a long time ago
the house is never clean because i am still alive, dirtying whatever i can
i confirm your worst fears about my personality: cunning, horny
busy signaling the bill collector, vomiting in country crock
a sunlit silo set in rows of wheat crops stares back from the bucket
this is how i terraform the silence: from the stomach
one shirt sleeve crusted in translucent bile, steadying myself
on hand-me-down pianos, squelching from the waist down
i call crying just to check what it sounds like on speaker
to terrorize a family dinner; this time, i don't expect help

ode to the father of my abortion

like lipstick on a limp dick
i left you cavalcading, full of sidewalk
congratulating your killer on the occasion of his first smashed sparrow

focus: some die for birth
yesterday we were giants, tomorrow we winter in place
i left you like this: the archangel of surge protectors

painstakingly translating my family photo into vanish
blow money, no more foul-mouthed music box
fight me if i try to wife the world

buy a gun, drive drunk, grow skeptical, steal fire
after it started—telling time by gag reflex
"hello" got too heavy, artists tend to leave

shadows last, autumn empty, sex obscure
accept this   international reacharound
after hate, i start to confuse dark ocean with your name

the last fool ever suffered

for the umpteenth cervical biopsy
warn me before the worms come

leave me a trail of beer bottles
to follow into unconsciousness

x-ray my toothless piping daily
implant new plastic behind my bones

some people want to get hit by a bus
but no, give me six months

at the edge of a paper table
for forgiveness from the ceiling panels

polluted starlight further diffused by dust
in the room allotted for bad news

i apologize to stained furniture
for suffering fools until i became one:

jumping turnstiles to impress drug dealers
leaving the cat alone too long, letting sour cream

rot in the sink, pinning the national debt on my parents
telling doctors they're the devil, whatever

there are apparently zero nerve endings in the cervix
so when i flinch at the hole punch, it's a miracle of modern science

i apologize   not for feeling it   but because i couldn't run

remember the empire

i don't mind being objectified
as a helicopter or a matchbook, in the right light, sparking sulfur
over rooftops i once swung a single leg off
into loose gravity like a fishing line
i don't mind turning vehicular
a stalled out metaphor out-of-breath pundits could never resist
i don't mind polygraphs or deductibles
or that state fair sound the freeway makes
under the overpass, i miss minding it
i miss feeling my fingers
under my shirt to keep warm
this is how people describe freezing to death:
i don't mind the cold anymore
i will remember the empire for its grave-deep dimples
gold chevys dipped in chocolate fountains
tanning bed stench of bleach and stomach acid
condoms swapped for sour candy
remember beanie babies, maybe, or the way
we made beauty halfway bionic, remember fringe technologies
like nail glue and pressed pill abortion

remember we clutched corroded earrings
and heard our grandmothers still singing
remember our last dollars spent on epiphany that never kicked in
that the sum total of life's meaning was recalculated in a financial app
and when we opened it, there was nothing left but unmatched socks
like a scene from a movie where teenage whimsy
suddenly forebodes something
our main character stares off camera, scared shitless
into a distance we aren't meant to witness
and we are left to guess: maybe finally
motion without friction, a restart button, the new religion

one-star review of human nature

the hearts of my enemies were undercooked again
god's tiny penis sang happy birthday to the table
without consent, a president got lost on the way
to the bathroom and pissed on a plastic plant
the parking lot is full of hot cars running since the 70s
with children in them, back when daddy rinsed his hands
in a restaurant alone, drowned out coked-up silence
with city water, quit dreams
by the time we arrived, there was nothing left to see
i broke my baby teeth out for this lawsuit
i asked for the manager to retire into a multi-level marketing scheme
after all i've been through, the least they could do is
empty everything, call me back with a check
the least anyone could do is call an ambulance
it's an emergency, how bored i get

caption america

this land mass is a gold-plated
coat hanger on which i drape nine wars
worth of ground meat, our most delicate keepsakes
little silver metal with a dead girl at the center
great lakes sucked onto aircraft crushed
into crystals pinned to bony chests
i rest in constant pilgrimage, in sunlit-to the-point-of-grief
anything but peace, anything but burnt in effing
jesus, an effigy tends to mean whatever smoke
happens to do to you when no one's looking
at the campfire someone expects fanfare, so it's
automatically there, and if i tell you a ghost story
cornered crawlers who once lived on this property
would rise up from gaped fissures in the cowering sidewalk
the spirit of the abandoned factory would depart
its cable-laden body and cover us with farming chemicals
orthogonal time itself might cry buckshot from its dali eye
so i stay quiet, change the subject from fiction to fiction
until i can't remember which one we call history
we spot new species of barbed creatures down the canyon

the next day and who's to say if renaming

kills more than creates?

bathroom graffiti summary of youth

for Garrett

under the church meetup sticker
we found out who to call for a good time
how to spell words like "blowjob," "motherfucker," "whore," "cuck"

outside, we watched half-empty powerade bottles
float down the river, chugged mickey's malt liquor
smashed the glass in gravel alleys, pretended to be drunk

the game was always "i spy what sullies the scene
with raw evidence of human existence" and it was easy:
approach any distant vista and just look for fast food wrappers

no down payment on the planet, we never cleaned the lookout
no idea you would disappear years later, from a familiar intersection
center of downtown, Planned Escape, Indiana, no one expected you to be

more raw evidence in the river, dragged out by kayaks we used to throw rocks at
in sunday best, with turned cheek, no one expected us to be anything
we thought we'd prove them all wrong, didn't we?

futurism in reverse

if, unlike the elders, who recall across shag-carpeted parlors a world before
flash animation and factory smokestacks, you think back, nostalgic about
a tagged seagull stealing a cheeto, a hollowed out computer monitor
big enough to fit your baby cousin, if the factories, now abandoned
menageries of broken glass, were enough memento of death
without stomping a single squirming starling in a burlap sack
if premade meatloaf under cellophane once felt like christmas
if the future itself is now past, replaying only by digitization
from VHS, if your childhood foreshadowed creeping cataclysm
and now you sell it as cheap prophecy, the oracle of deluge
if you've grown sick of old men's stories, the principle of which
is always "fish swallow each other," if you can feel yourself evolving
a quiet mutant, if you can read this right now with new amphibious limbs
if silence were attainable, we would have tried it one time and hated it

woe to the alpha and the omega

spread the unholy gospel
tell anyone who will listen:
resist hierarchy

i'm texting my ex again
he sent me a screenshot of a wikipedia article
about the *omegaverse*

(look it up after this)
i responded *incel-adjacent*
male-gazey, something about *penis envy*

i said: listen, i'm a different person
in bed, i don't identify as *submissive*
anymore, i don't tell anyone

how bad it got before words worked
one surly morning, the omega
will devour the alpha

the working class will rise up
the meek will inherit whatever is left
woe to those who believe themselves alpha

for they will abominate the numberless
woe to those who believe themselves omega
for they shall bow to sleepless daddies

birds are already yelling about dawn
and we are still awake collecting stray
prison experiments in our back pockets

it's morning and it's not even trendy to be sad anymore
it's morning in the omegaverse and i'd rather be waterboarded
it's morning and it's not a metaphor for any cock crow

of enlightenment or salvation
resist hierarchy
it's only morning due to distant explosions

friendly fire from on high

the good news is there's no good news

only sunlight, the perpetual revolt, still crying

FULL SERPENT

once worshipped

local legend says you swallowed yourself whole
    sterile swap-out, avatar for avatar
but everyone knows better than to believe starlight

on the well-worn path of winking mutants
    there is no more cocaine to speak of
some drugs got old a long time ago, so we wait

for new ones to fall through the sewer grate
    sift through dirty snow for fresh smokable wonder
tits out pontificating about the transits of rogue planets—family

fanned out like an asteroid belt, too distant to count
    a finger-point on clear nights and that's it
all you get—the rest must rot, or else

it wouldn't be real enough to burrow deep in the blood vessel
    and live there through winter, wedged in the underground tunnels
full of dead gods, and i know they want me stormed apart

and i know i want it, too

hymn to exes

prayer:

may all your reckless impulses
amass to make
a sacred home among daredevils

curse:

may it hurt
may it hurt so fucking much
the damage can't forget your face

prayer:

to satan or to no one
to dumpster pigeons
who lived or didn't
(no one checked)

curse:

if trapped, the lids loosen
a little too late for you
the insides of learned rooms
clog with vestigial wings

prayer:

for prisons to peel off the world
like the skin of an overripe fruit
its tart juices aimed at the moon

curse:

to drown in it, the entire ocean
filling up an astronaut helmet
watch: the gold wheel headed somewhere
better off without you

prayer:

and when the deluge ends (again)
pulling the wet seeds from your hair
in all the languages that carry
they'll whisper what they think you meant

curse:

they will be wrong
the skinless fruit next sheds its flesh
the power systems hum inhumanly
it's delicious when you're gone

the hierophant hosts a dinner party

everything is almost ready: hell is in the oven
heaven halved and gutted
the tradition is to feel nothing, but he can't help it
the illuminati of the colorless earth are all here
business-faced, unlistening, with their backs to the machine
whatever they're eating sports an undercarriage like an insect
instead of grace, they say something later redacted, later erased
the last course is served on a need-to-know basis
wriggling, red-pink, still alive at the center
uncanny, how blood sacrifice changes shape but never goes away
the circle of satellite orbit and the circle of the headless chicken
intersect like a corporate logo
street artists reimagine it as testicles or tits, of course
and for all we know, that's what it stands for
for all we know, the meaning of life is to bone

the red room where no one ever gets what they want

the next morning, i am always surprised by what i find
in the red room where no one ever gets what they want

except us, except when people cheat the coordinates
into thinking they don't intersect—i bet you'd guess

we'd never fall for that, the whole-hearted hand-hold
famished chapel—in fact, we'd be the first to laugh

into the grenade of godlessness, strip off the sequined hints
rinse down an avalanche with even more collapse

love is letting the snow obstruct your airways and
pin your frozen skeleton to the side of a mountain

unless it isn't, unless we've been tricked
we plan a trip north of the sewer to see the sky again

and that's enough church for one lifetime
i go back to fucking so loud neighborhood dogs answer

their wild snouts shaking like drunk guns
hind legs scraped shut—i am coming

to the sound of the oven telling me it's over
but after dinner, even underground

we are still starving to be buried

the joke

in the joke, a bar walks into america and never walks out
it isn't very funny, unless, of course, you were there

even the hot springs are private property now
we scale a mountain with bum knees just to watch

the spas get richer, the south freeze over
the parks ever so slowly dividing by paywall

i wish we could relish the joke for what it is:
the story of rootlessness mixing a drink

at the nexus of new violence, growing up alongside
chain link, with a punchline buried at the edge

like a landmine, like a war far from home—
but instead, it's only a social experiment

to see if anyone might laugh, and they don't

playing with plague

we were once much smaller than kids come now
allowed to balance beam our bare feet on steel bed frames
zero supervision, and the TVs shouting HIV, and the ocean in a can
and the caravan to barbie's house at the top of the back stairs

when ken got sick, we couldn't tell at first; our mouths mumbled
platitudes like in the documentaries, like on the news
we drew his lesions in sharpie, drove him to doctors
simulated kisses with the frozen grins of friends

we'd already imagined a mansion that generates infinite money
a treehouse made of orange peels, a system for making our hands smell
like summer, but never once did he survive, because that was how it
was back then; we might imagine, but we would never lie

songs i know

song of loose wolves, song of hungry dollars
song of hotboxed erotics on train tracks
song of pregnant cravings for termination
song of bluebells with their poisoned tongues out
song of staredown, song of stalking
song of oversized clothing caught in chain link
song of jailbait braiding the constellations into tiny outfits
song of paid sex, song of abstinence, song of pressing bare tits
against my phone camera over facetime, song of long distance
song of jellyfish descending onto the beach like overcharged
transmission towers, song of the sheltered kid and song of the cynic
song of return to a watery hometown, but dylan is dead
song of the past caving in on itself, song of the not-felt-yet
song of surprise at just how much can be thrust in the throat
before the body rejects it, song of foreign airports
song of giving the 911 operator bad directions
song of brainwash, song of brimstone, song of having killed someone
on the way home, song of lucid nightmare, of having lived long enough
head hung sick out the car window, but hey, i know this song
it played the night the world burned down—you know it?
go ahead, you sing the melody; i'll find the third up and jump in

crystal disc

on the car ride into the canyon you dream
a crystal disc where worst memories could spin
externally, labeled things like
"dad leaving," "catholic school," "car wreck"
you'd take them out, full serpent
flashbacks be damned, splashed through
with rainbow light, the weight of them
like folded paper that might frisbee into flight
their flimsy technology enters your obsolete body
but just for the night, just for the slim segment of eternity
when you need to say everything
out loud, right now, to any insect in earshot
you'd shout out only what you could put back on the shelf
and wake up half erased, redacted
almost clean, almost unraped

belief in evil

when you believe in evil, steaks don't taste right
lilacs collapse under the weight of dumbstruck fungus
little girls still hide, like i did, from pickup trucks in the park
after dark, new crop tops snagged in brambles but half repaired
down the block—nobody's watching, until you don't want it
then they're everywhere, resewing the flowers and asking what happened
so you say *evil,* beware of dog, a bad man is easy to find
and all the aftermath nods knowingly, like it's normal for escape
to feel as narrow as the throat mid-swallow, mid-throwup
people who believe in evil tend to believe it lives here
in the gut, with the rest of the engines we've forgotten
how to take apart—parasitic, sick with secrets, past quick fixing
at dusk now, we lock the doors to shut it out, but it doesn't work
i don't believe in evil, and if i did, i have already worn it thin

hallowed be the whores

to my neighbor who was offered a $20 BJ on our street during pandemic
to my sister and craigslist and all its rabid gods who aren't in heaven
to julia and maya and rachel and the clubs that kept them awake
on molly and lucy and tina and the promise of parties that pay
to the barbie doll who broke my hymen so i might feel no pain
in the valley of the shadow of first sexual encounters amen

hallowed be the whores, the sugar babies, strippers, porn stars, cam girls
escorts, freestylers—hearts of gold, cold hustle, whom i owe by the dozen
hallowed be the word of the whore, for i believe her over anyone
hollered over too-loud new wave or whispered in the bathroom
may she drink champagne in paradise, may she indulge
every temptation, may she deliver us from cloistered lives

at least an hour, fully compensated, as it is written, as it persists
may she devour us whole-hearted or leave only what the crows
could snatch easily, may she break bread with angels at midnight
tint her cheeks with fresh cherries, may she rearrange the world
as she sees fit and then tell us all about it, may she forgive us our
trespasses and then remember and laugh and then wink at the camera

our father, whoever the fuck you are
it's my eyelash stuck to hers, we know exactly what we've done

all money is drug money

don't overthink it:
side views of men's heads have always
chiseled themselves into heavy metals
hard labor has always been cheap
if the nightmare has a dreamer
he's been dead too long to matter
inherited repeatedly like bad jewelry
and on the playground, at the funeral
i've never met a set of siblings who agreed
on what to sell and what to keep

very whatever

homeward bound and gagged
i once thought sex would never get dull
i thought the spirit was shaped like a watermelon seed
i thought the devil lived in a holographic jewelry box i kept in my closet
a collection of razor blades swiped from my father
expired condoms, sometimes ecstasy or vodka
too small by high school, the container kachina-dolled
into a payless sarcophagus: old prescriptions
pocket knives, pregnancy tests, unpassable notes
i fed him every day and the devil grew large enough to burst
lick of fire stretching my elastic eardrum and i listened for impact
like so much depended on a glass-eyed dragon
meaningless bookend on my parents' dresser that i associated with satan
very whatever, staring everywhere at once like a marble, like the
county fair on mushrooms, ferris wheel still spitting seizures
but the bone-crunch never came—i made the whole thing up
or else perhaps the dungeon swells in silence and
we are all stuck in its stomach

my mother informs me everyone has horses

today i sent my family an AI-generated obituary
"she had no horses, but thought she did," it read
"everyone has horses," my mother replied, and i laughed
in the language of acres uncounted

from starter apartment to starter apartment
at the outskirts of the city, biking to save money
my neighbors' toddler climbs onto their chihuahua's back
and smacks its haunches with a playskool frisbee like a drunk jockey

my mother has never owned horses
but she can hand-draw the difference between a trot, canter, and gallop
pronounces *dressage* correctly, sobs over Black Beauty
waxes nostalgic about Mr. Ed, so i responded

"sure, the kind you hold when told to be patient
or perhaps the kind beaten long after death"
some obsolete proverb for "too soon" or "too late"
if horse is a code word, i can find it in the shadow of

the interstate with whatever cash we have left tonight
but no, that isn't what mom meant
she said, "everyone *thinks* they have horses, at least
and in the end, isn't that the same thing?"

citizens of what

yes i am almost ready
for this dog-eared town
to spit us out
here, the stomach locks itself
from the inside
whosoever suggested we start
swallowing keys?
the churches dress down now
as if to go undercover
as if to camouflage the guardrail
i imitate their certain furrow
in the mirror at night like
my arrest is solid sermon
lice have scurried so long
across this skull country
and i've befriended every one of them
we are the citizens of something
rumbling in the plumbing
paper cups the city drops
draped bandage-delicate
we still stand out against the businessmen
and choir ladies in this deli
our necks crane different
at smoking helicopters overhead
be the unbothered turkey breast
you wish to see in the world, i guess
i'll be bothered enough for the both of us
nibbling the last bits of biome off the bone
i don't usually eat meat, but today is an occasion

commemorated by unflinching wings
we are leaving in a wet heave
no one will live at this address
the mail will all return to sender
they'll wonder only for a moment where we went

gap in the static

at the end of the radio, fuzz pedal presidents found dead
i lick the whole substrate into orbit, where is your horny god now?
no one really cares, but there's a storm coming, internet in and out
we fiddle with electronics like the word of some slumlord
might come through any moment, with the coordinates of whatever
missiles fixate on next: the criminal ways we've fed the cats
house arrests, home videos, empty coke vials decorating closets
i was stuck there once, next to the air conditioning vent
and a lot of us imagined outer space
and a lot of us went there, and a lot of us stayed

beta haze

i left my keys in the pockets of my old skin
the only detail i missed, the rest are no different
space keeps eating itself in perfect spiral formation
photographs keep nodding knowingly toward posterity
as if there is any, as if we could go on like this indefinitely
with dust bowls pooling in our work boots and the sun about to pop
i light up radioactive like a cursed gemstone
and that's all i hope for—the future doesn't flirt back
i accept this strikeout as my most godlike attribute
former things fade away for my sole entertainment
home awaits the displacement of our outlined little handprints
the secret to enlightenment is not giving a shit

the world drain

is this the deadend you were looking for?
the hitchhiking stormfront, pearl skeleton
midwest farmhouse wide awake to char its harvest
we blow a tire, romance a downed power line
set off detroit's booby traps, puke up a perfect sunset
i introduce you to whoever's left, pull a rusty nail
from my thrift store boot like a magic trick
smoke a blunt in the parking lot and all the angels come
to eat me out—i no longer fear god, but i fear the fog
she fucked to get us here, i fear the smiling coyote
who lives in your silence, i even fear the neon of I-55
when it's bright enough to blind the sun and i can't find you
in the passenger's seat anymore, i can't find anyone
to stretch the world drain wide enough to flush
so i just sit there in the toilet water, under the lightswitch
of misspent disappearance, almost envious
of all the lost objects that never put up any fuss

vetting the ether

you don't hear this word anywhere but poetry:
ether, outdated intoxicant, open air that lies so vacant
it could devour bone marrow, a vagueness of
stormscape somewhere past the upper atmosphere
wherever it is, i've never seen it, almost by
definition, almost by design, a neat little spot
to tuck whatever extra a reader might want:
last gods left standing, all the bodies at the bottom
of the dock, grandmother's stocking, a wedding
full of moths—i'm sorry for showing them off:
the little trinkets i have nowhere to stuff
except the ether, with its tentacled perfume
wrapped around your worst fear, i'm so sorry
but i'm told one look at the ether is worth it
so i'm taking a walk down by the river tonight and—
well, it won't take long—you wanna come?

liminal brothel

i used to keep my shed scabs in a piggy bank, then a music box
then an urn for someone else's mother
people told me it was morbid, but how then shall we live
if not by dead shreds? the fridge overflows with them
the taxidermist subsists by market demand
i refuse to clean anything soon to be smithereens
generations of beasts minded their own destruction
before it was any of our madness, but now starving
is a trademarked business, a pious grift, a ponzi scheme
we save the scraps to prove, yes, the old gods can still kill us
one of them writhes under my dress to this day
but others we banish to secondhand containers
we never open, peering into the coin slot once a year
eyeless until moment of contact, scaleless until rotted loose

minutia trenches

zoomed in like this, the scales uncouple
sex is a zeno's paradox:
the proximity is electric but
we never really touch

claw machine of eternal cocktease
i live for the motion sickness, grope to drop
button smashed with both hands, quarters clacking
knowing full well no one gets what they want

i met you on an island, teetering edge of the country
and i almost fell right off, and you almost caught me
but no, that would require contact, an alien concept
instead, i trampoline off the dock, interpenetrated by the tongues of

subatomic stuff—to know is to be fucked, and then to look up
and find the watch dogs unconscious, door unlocked
to feed raw honey and guts to any insect who knocks
to feel the hive inside you writhe—not union quite, but close enough

give up like you mean it

why don’t you carry me down the staircase in my absolute ugly?

bald spot and spider vein, chipped manicure and flaked lipstick

i relish the way things fade with age, any age, even an hour

that the flesh the church condemned is more engine than shelter

i secretly love all the leakage, nascent volcanoes spewing infection

heaven is just a term we invented for when everything is over

pus extracted, incision sewn shut, and it feels like before you were born

when the mad hawks didn’t scream and you didn’t miss them

and the sounding boards just buzzed incessantly—carry me there

in your cracked talons, with glitter soap in my mouth, oh my god

i am so turned on by the worst case, last ditch, gasped angst

like the faucet as we left it in the house: hot as hellfire pouring forth

erotics of the soapbox

when you're on top, talk like a desperate prophet
warn of horses and their flushed riders portending rapture
one day the ocean will crack open like a music box, like my jaw
at the dentist, and you will have predicted it, spitting your scrolls into
the back of my throat every night as you pretend to rest, but really
your lips are busy drafting next frames before they happen
no one questions why revelations flock to the soapbox
and nowhere else, but that's how we met, on the curb outside
some pizza shop, a familiar tale: the wooden prop, handheld
restaurant, the three-act play of sex, starting with the soapbox and ending
wherever the pale horse says   *get off*   and we do
but not before spoiling the ending of the universe
not before coaxing the floodwaters straight out of our bones
we know this story already, not from any sacred text, but from
the street and all its pulpits curling world history into a fist

the art of fact

for Chris

bridges aren't built to get over it
in your grandmother's basement, you watched
a coyote eat the last bee and laugh

you found a ship in a bottle, dropped acid
30 years later to deep-clean my
first solo apartment, and then asked

"do you remember?" but as kids, we lived a jetstream apart
our mothers still couldn't pick each other out of a lineup
i have never stepped foot inside your former californias

so i laughed with all my teeth, hallucinating a room of doilied
rocking horses and toothpicked foremasts, but yes, before we die
i confess, i do remember

i'm your imaginary friend
balanced in glass, anchored mid-brain
i was there for the construction of the lake you can't escape

i twitched my wings across the peeling paint of your solitary
confinement, i circuited the electricity for this conversation to take place
i am the god in the machine of manic pixelated demonology

that governs us, yes, i saw the ship in a fucking bottle
and it was beautiful, i think they made it just for us
never to get over—what intricate ashtrays

to feed the sea someday, maritime mime in miniature
floating upside down into the sunset, rippled gunshot mirage
and that's what you wanted, right?

for me to say, yes, we dosed the same amount
i recognize you in the ridiculous rib cage of history
standing in some gusty kitchen with the lights out, half drunk

one testicle peeking out the cathedral door of your boxers
you reread a postcard that puts you in a limousine
rocketing over the monotonous gray of lake pontchartrain

it's frozen that way, folded from the wallet in your back pocket
and you spend another evening wondering what bobs in the water
right beside us: an alligator, a paper bag

a human body, a transmission tower
in the picture, you are on lookout forever
anyone can buy your face

the black box records our defanging

have you heard
the gnashings of the former feral
the skin drop, midair
failed parachute of hospital sheets
have you watched
an insect stun itself with light
and lie down supine
under circling sparrows
have you smelled the wreckage
thrust your fingers into the throat
of a choking child
checked the pulse of apparent luck
well of course not
mother taught by example
“death is women’s work”
a solo ascent to a summit
too cold for some to stomach
thousands of visits with flowers
a musical arrangement of warships
someone must cradle the car-crushed
last breaths of stray kittens
even if it means running into traffic
we weigh the dangers, the mountain
by now familiar, and decide that
we were born here
terror had held us all along

NO ONE IS DADDY

vcr's last words

i miss when home movies were shitty
i felt so seen and heard by satan
those wavy lines that would keep moving even when it was paused
the trick of using a butter knife to wind the tape back up
why is it so unbelievable

to have witnessed the end of era after era like a vampire
to see a pileated woodpecker next to a prison in michigan
and think, *without pictures, history is meaningless*
no one will know i was here, basic bitch of bird watching
without binoculars, just inches from the rumble strip

dumb luck, happy accident, another moment
whose poignance feels more like a morbid joke i don't get yet
because i'm not quite dead enough
but just you wait, i'm lying down in lots of pentagrams
and praying to the planets, i'm growing scales on both my eyes

to then slough off, i live by a strict schedule
of scribbles in the blank space
i kiss the tv and the static stings my tongue
now i understand why kids stick forks into electrical outlets
to meddle in the source of magic, to meet the beast behind the hum

fossil of desire

even in the dark, boogie man panting
i pretend there are cameras planted all around me
documenting the delicate sighs of the damned

in reality, some basements stay lonely
every sink in the house overflows unnoticed
i am a claustrophobic cave painting created by serial

monogamists with a death wish
hold the door open for bees to fly into my bedroom
even lilies have sex with themselves if they can

and if not, their stigma will visibly
drip nectar until it stains your table
i'm not kidding when i say the rain remembers

the stickiness contains the fossil of desire
mom and dad know this, it's mundane
people fuck and fuck off every day

sometimes i don't wash my sheets for weeks
and all the fabric becomes forensics
trailing evidence for plot points blacked out or

forgotten at the last address
deep in the stomach of the structure of a girl
this flower eats the stinger whole

hail mary, no one is daddy

between the siren wails at equal intervals
in our separate little cordoned off catacombs
we hear tires screech over and over
but no collision, like someone's doing donuts
in an empty intersection, daring anyone in charge
to stop them—the new normal is criminal
whiplash, reckless tonguing subway turnstiles
i drop my fibroid spittle in the center of wall street
and wait two weeks for the future to incubate
anticlimax of bored biology passing around
half-dead RNA strands, i'm afraid to lift the dumpster lid
without gloves, water the plants without a bandana
over my nose and mouth, the fountains stop pumping
the salons close up shop, no backyard boils
this crawfish season, but we still porch-sit six feet apart
raise our rye from afar, trash-talk tone-deaf spring breakers
sext our exes, learn to work from home
plant root vegetables, calculate the risk of getting sick
if one day we come to miss the phenomenon of fucking
too much to resist, swallow the rest of the acid for kicks
i wake up the next day to a beetle tickling my ankle
and its backend has those little pincers and i kill it
with my favorite boot: high-heeled, black suede and
full of grace at the hour of death amen

yes all censors

under the cockeyed cover of a cartoon flower
redaction made flesh, incision turned technicolor
i picture myself draped in the negligees
of animal banishment, fishnets streaming bycatch
my quantum body is only illegal if someone sees it
plucked bloody from the edges of the screen
grand unboxing where i emerge so naked
my thin skin is erased without a word
made anything, without a single
surface left to smithereen

the fallacy of daddy

the fallacy of enlightenment lasted a fallacy of time we don't talk about

the fallacy of dreamcatchers gave way to the fallacy of leeches gave way to

the fallacy of antibiotics gave way to the fallacy of radiation and it's still raining

reasons to fall ass-first into conspiratorially branching antlers

the fallacy of ashtrays leads you to the fallacy of cancer leads you to

the fallacy of recovery, but they're all too slippery to land on for long

the fallacy of solid ground is swallowed by the fallacy of magma

is swallowed by the fallacy of mountains is swallowed by the fallacy of god

the fallacy of fathers, the fallacy of apples gone bad by not falling far enough

pick up the rot by the stem and the rest drops right back, incredulous mush

fallacy of earthworm, fallacy of afterlife as vaguely sentient space dust

the waking state is always when the dream feels weirdest

fallacy of alarm clock, fallacy of happenstance clairvoyance

and then the ships start disappearing even in pictures

retroactive dazzle stealth mode, fallacy of trust

history talking to itself

when all the expensive speakers power down, you can hear history talking to itself

awkward standstill, misplaced trailblaze, careful catalogue of red flags

softened by star spangle, the library of congress lives to forget its contents

if you were loved by the bard, i'm sorry, but he was mistaken

words immortalize no one, here now and then gone, cuneiform or computer server

whatever drug you're on will wear off by dawn, when there are always inexplicable

feathers all over the point of departure, and you remember only enough to guess

a renaissance of interspecies understanding happened here in your unwashed

bedsheets with the little flowers that look like they're wilting but it's just the angle

a certain primal dance they know and you don't and you hate them for it

their disappearing lilac bunched under a blood stain that fades for decades

but it's still there in the dim glow of portage avenue, where i'm home for christmas

every year but this one, and you tell me things are different now

but if i took your word for it, you'd be wrong

the canker veil

to mistake the rain for a body shaking with laughter is one thing
i hope i never get over. another is your long-lost leather and liquorice
aesthetic, hanging half out the passenger's seat window, middle of nowhere
moment in america when we hadn't pulled back the canker veil yet
whom we might marry was a glittery question mark kicking with hot sex
galloping reunions in airports, obligations made easy by the touch of
the same solid soldier every night, snoring a song only you recognize
but today, mid-city is eerily quiet, the neon signs flicker desperately
to stay with us before shutting off. life is a sentence with no question left
so we serve it to each other, back and forth across the courtyard
wave to strangers through an iron fence from the bottom of our shriveled hearts
dig up the diamond rings we saved from former engagements and try them on
curious whether the past still fits, perfectly snug over the knuckle
and it almost does, but the fitful metallic embrace we cartoon doodled
as kids strangles now, the kettle beeps three times instead of screaming
i paint my face for war before braving the outdoors, and when it's over
all i see is exoskeleton, a turning inside out, six astonished continents
wriggling on their backs, waiting for the birds or the mercy of a heavy
footfall to finish them off. falling in love is a pastime of atmospheres
younger than this, confiscated by the authorities, controlled substance
of the gut, trying over and over, against all odds, to keep failing up

lay-off lilies

witchcraft is whatever i make of my wilting lay-off lilies

arctic ablaze, condolence pestled down into a poultice

requested dropper of your blood, wide-eyed with ingredients

buzzing with bored atoms, ergot and motherwort shook in like candy

i am only sorry i didn't leave a hexed apple in a desk drawer

enunciate the old gaelic of cliffside ancestors over the intercom

i am only a collection of loose seeds crushed together in the stomach

the nausea is temporary, the hallucinations are permanent

you won't believe all the bees coming to pollinate the heads of state

you cannot count the hordes of insects crossing over-patrolled borders

the spell is what goes undetected in the medicine of street vendors

tendrils of plant matter conquering the back porch without consequence

it's the music always emanating even from still, frictionless meat

at the myth of family dinner, with its fervent blessing over slaughter

what can perish

so what's next? after first freakout
reinvest your roth in gold and stock up on nonperishables?

nest egg for the apartment because you're not allowed to leave it
we thought armageddon would be one thing:

the heat, galactic collision, runaway gods come home to roost
but it's everything: cleared throat in the boardroom

honeybee under my boot, stench around st. rose, louisiana
i've saved a little money for when university degrees go back

to their original lives as tree pulp, for when my bosses
finally read my poetry, for when the system blows over in strong wind

no revolution necessary—the top-heavy odds will take care of it
we track the numbers of global and local infected

like we can cost/benefit a way out, map a route someplace else
hitch our trailer to the twilight zone, but no

such love, no such sweet carrion, despite our deepest wishes
we keep existing, nonchalant crisis after nonchalant crisis

sometimes i am sick and tired of being a lawful citizen
sometimes i unhook all the fasteners of my outfit

and let the breeze comb through my ghost cloud
the contagious never touch, but i would risk it

under the right barbed wire, crescent gap-toothed
smiling, i would place your palm on what can perish

and let you feel the muscled engine wrenching
oceanic in its monsters, faster and faster

exhibitionist's nocturne

i walk around with no underwear or curtains when i want attention
spot a neighbor at the iron-wrought gate of my nightmare and wave

whosoever stares back long enough turns crystal into powder into pressed pill
hypnosis doesn't work unless you're already down the drowsy spiral

hunt inside yourself—gunshot for breakfast, shoreless swim out at night
unprotected sex with strangers whose faces filter the city into a mirror ball

i remember their names, like the rest of history, only because
they are written down, neatly organized in temporal order

with annotations on context, optional patronymics
i lie wide awake, pretend i am sleeping prey, and survey those who strike:

what is the taste of the meat you miss most? the backseat, the attic, twisted
hand-hold over the banister—i insist you're sentimental when you do it

follow the sound of your own fangs piercing my empty fists without argument
in the lavender half-light, i'm thinking of all this when i see you

through the window before dawn, when it's still too dark
to notice, and you don't look up, not once

the former order

for what felt like an eternity, nobody imagined me in rum-soaked sheets
singing through a smoke-haunted esophagus into a broken air conditioner

there was a silver box lined with blotter paper for the aftermath of any emotion
there was a curdled substance building under the entire structure

not all the landlords smelled yet, the stray cats still came to us
we ate cookies high above the street and shared the secrets

melting in our pockets since elementary, when danger was a man's name
like mine, an efficient criminal who thrilled loose animals to ruin

since then, i've lived up to it: the drum tap of dare atop dare until
the crescendo threatens to deafen—the blizzard of base lived experience

with no spam filter, exhausted to its conclusion: money was so tired
it slept for two months, is just now waking up, i hibernated

heat-free, deep in the grass, gathering the right roots to sustain me
until the equinox came like a call to arms—anyone's, sun-scarred and

circumscribing, a tattoo on one forearm of a family seal, the wax still
dripping all night long, the former order melted down into a kissed, familiar fear

epoch the likes of which

wider, now—the tiny colony that sustains your celebrity is watching

well-hung couriers who bike bottles of wine across cities on sundays

under blue laws just to seduce, and you let them, because what is the use

in waiting on bridges to unzip the river? what is forever in the trench?

on appointment days, you hide out in the shower before and after

war, mom's words, glitter, semen—a few things that never wash off

but they might this time, you tell yourself, with the water pressure

cranked full blast against the back of your head, lazy ashes and fruit flies

dropping through your vitreous humor like a flashback doing weather

effects for the present—you check the mirror when it's over

hightail the towel, pry back the eyelash, and oh my god

lo and behold: there is no person anymore

print out my insides

my former feelings are now available for instant download as a pdf
locked for edits, falsely colorized black hole time-stamped by nasa

my cells have since recycled the rape straight out of my body but
they're still alive on google drive, anxious to be opened up, gawked at

submitted for piecemeal publication, reported to corporate
divided among a thousand local servers tracing dropped lumps

of scar tissue back to their owners: "are you still watching?"
"did you forget to attach to something?" the answer is all over

the internet but i still don't know it by heart, so i look it up:
the master file of human violence deemed safe enough for work

and yes, i'm still there, failing to paperclip the pond scum back into my hair
i'm so accessible within the document, your email might as well find me dead

//

in shallow water, like you wanted
the night i printed out my insides

to hang in the attic and you spotted
at long last, the worm

curling into knots until it popped
and you decided the wind needed

a new wig, which you threw to it
overhead, not guessing what

i'd throw next, with the flick of a fist:
former feelings, reams and reams of them

carried to cooler cities on hooting storms
i'm sorry for a lot of things, but not for

//

most days, once the chickadees were awake, linen curtains leaning in, letting the worm sun itself, minding the silence, sheep's head always turned to speak, spliff by the river, passed out in piss, lips to someone else's drink, the tops of lungs like helicopters over a mesa, leaving your letter in the mailbox for days, touching the interface like i might stay, something solid, indigestible, unsearchable, the document saying "redact me. redact me." i am sorry for a lot of things but not for what hurts most: all that loose leaf, choking out an electrical transformer, the way the lightning rushed to meet the mouth you never could believe, the carburetor clicking colder, cattle startled, i am never sorry for letting weather spread cheap copies of my guts over the interstate. i am never sorry for the worst worms, through whom i am continually reborn. i am never sorry for zipping the photos up and going public, for keeping a sliver of that old lightning in a corked jar on my desktop, to take out and taste when i'm waxing nostalgic, to exhaust into submission until it strikes me from a standstill again and again, just the same as it did then, when i watched in astonishment the letters of your name fly weightless into space without complaint, simultaneously saved and erased

between commercials

toss me a beer from the near future. tie the loose strings of your bathing suit to mine.
describe sex as a vector determining the positions of relative parasites. tell me again
how heartbreak is like being high all the time on a drug you hate. tell me the forest
can't quit smoking, that there were never stars where you grew up, but 30 minutes
outside every mid-country city, there they are: in some church parking lot, with your
headlights off, silence except for soft stereo music and coyotes you mistake for ghosts.
no one mentions the divorce, but that doesn't stop outer space from rewiring itself
while we're asleep, which requires wind to howl incessantly through sterile air filters
and in the morning, the house feels like a funeral for someone you never met
or the night after your best friend's dad left for cigarettes. god lives between commercials
for the brief moment of dead air that lingers in the ear after it's over, signature silence
his greatest hit. talk over it, raid the fridge, pierce my skin in a pinch. anything but
the old tunnel with its held breath, restless vomit. pray the tv raises me, like hell
to taste the tip of every opening, inanimate valves hissing steam. pray, if you must,
that i'm taken peacefully to the prison of my dreams, that it's a situation comedy

of which i was never the lead, that god forgot us for good reason, that the front porch is still thick with jasmine on the day designated for noticing such things. and if it isn't then i'm sorry: the wishing well is full of bird shit. if it still worked, i would live in it sticky with old coins, collecting iridescent beetles. under the deepest watermarks of the world's wants, i'd be completely prayed away

textbook anomaly

going home hurts my throat now
glass half dead cat, photos too
exposed to know what happened

someone upstairs insists
there is another term for praying
the rosary (impossible to recall

impossible to rule out)
and the rest of the night is solid
goose chase into catechism

smashing translucence in case it's faking
tip of the tongue lost in laundry
like some jeans pocket

jingles the sacred heart of the joke
folded into filmy erasure, but in the morning
we admit there's no such language

half-remembered from a field guide to
the american southwest, what matters is
we knew we were mistaken all along

we checked, in fact: the sinkhole
in the dictionary isn't big enough
for church words to drop down

what matters is it doesn't matter
the hunt for nothing sounds fun
with our dinky little flashlights

flipping the property blind dark
to blind white, wedged between revelations
blinked into heavy mascara

all around us, vinca invisibly attempts
photosynthesis on a 9-volt battery
wheels get dizzy with their own reinvention

coming home is like that
complex machinery rubbed pink
drunk again under the floorboards

old blood clots saved under the sink
heart-shaped boxes full of baby teeth
i pinch their soft spots, bone by bone

nine cavities whispered into cellophane
call it the carnage of the nursery
bartering glass beads for edible wings

there, another name for praying the rosary
new search results for all our meathooks
strung up like christmas in the land of disbelief

tongue-tied telos

after the incident at the capitol, we wash down brownies with
cheap bourbon and name all the cities in europe and canada
we wouldn't live together—picket fences reserved now for satire
or marxist critiques of some novel—after all, what would we possibly do

with that much stupid, schmaltzy heaven? to change the lightbulbs
mid-waltz, dig up long-garaged radios when the power shuts off
to ride a hunch into a well-worn ditch and pitch a flag there
basin bridge be damned, our bodies dumped into the risk

what's the point of settling down, if you'll have to claw back out?
but ah, the countryside of france, forgotten deserts of nuclear
test sites—if you could save us, you would have by now
but we still have to ask, formally, in writing, one last time

before we give up our longitudinal research on the self-parody of hope
and call it like we've seen it so far: a series of blast zones that work until they don't

cities i won't live in

new york is a nightmare
l.a. is someone else's dream
chicago is a scare tactic
houston is a c-suite barbecue
memphis is a rusted warehouse
detroit, an arsoned mechanic
boston is a non-rhotic language
san francisco is a computer virus
salt lake city doesn't drink enough
new orleans chugs puddles of unidentifiable liquid
minneapolis has an anxious attachment to its sibling
philly needs cheese whiz rehab
portland got so weird it lost the thread
austin only got weird enough to sell those threads on depop
denver made weed about capitalism
seattle made downers about death
san diego is a bait-and-switch for very sad whales
miami is where the mob dumps blackmailed bodies
orlando is a branded entity trademarked by a cutesy nazi
america is where i hide my head under brushfire
under roadkill, under bullets shot skyward at double weddings
call it provincial, call it postmodern whiplash
to wish the city on creatures more comfortable with blown covers
call it a symptom of some up-and-coming pathology
an aversion to ambition, an allergy to eavesdropping
call it anything but a tourist destination
sell me anything but a direct flight home
as soon as there is one, it won't be home anymore

let evil in

lace doesn't last long in this place
fingers get careless and the eyelets
come undone in dangling strips
but i don't get upset
i tell myself it's all tentacles anyway
even sisters talk each other into things with fists
after my first blowjob i ran off
into an already harvested cornfield
very specific indiana trauma, i joke at the bar
but it isn't, and at least one person usually gets it
locking eyes is dangerous, but we let ourselves
in tiny doses, on a rolling basis, as we deserve it
tattered underwear used to have better stories
rooftops whose storefronts blocked direct onlookers
beaches abandoned past sunset—at 2 in the morning
i make a stranger cum over the phone and hang up
swaggering at the extravagance, the very concept
of employment by a monster who admits it for once
no more office politics, department funding tug-of-war
just a voice in my ear telling me to open my body
and let evil in, hail satan, may the nighttime win

dawn's dropped jaw

when we meet at the hotel, don't tie me up just yet
wait for all entrances and exits to glow rosy

the bartender will realize, no, i'm not your daughter
there is no relation, the screaming stops like clockwork

at 3 in the morning, i'll call a ride by myself, leave separate
and on the drive, i'll imagine you not cleaning up

because everything's paid for, the rest of retirement
new pussy and tennis courts, in a different universe

my apartment of trash comforts: paper print-outs and secondhand blankets
but it's only up the block, in fact it's like i never left—yes, that's it

everyone acts like i'm so bad, drinking cognac with my shirt off
but i've done worse with one hand cuffed

to bathroom plumbing behind my back, i've done worse just for fun
for the dawn's dropped jaw, for no money at all

loves under construction

jackhammer of literality left behind at the gas pump
i sympathize with ecosystems that just give up
puddles of indeterminate gross-out fluids
the whole range of sensations nerve endings can't communicate

no doubt, there will be infinite renovations to whatever we once called the heart
scaffolds and chain-link fences will tell us which chambers to evacuate when
the fresh paint will reek with a finger-wagging forbiddance
but as in all our favorite legends, we won't obey

signage be damned, trespass happens for the sake of itself
what rabid curiosity it takes to evaporate
at one point, i ask you to take my picture with your belt around my neck
a stand-in for everything that stings, and you do it as if it's nothing but

two children standing at the edge of carnage
debating whether or not to swim

searchlight

the first time i sucked a dick for money, i wore the same knit black skirt

as when i met your mother for brunch on her back deck, drank fresh-squeezed

still-hot november out of your cupped hands like eggshells and the yolk stuck

to our chins—no one can quite say what i do now in public or under the private

surveillance of family, where the houses stand still in a way they never will for us

cover stories quilt the night in busy fabrics that clash at the seams

later, we sit naked before a floor-length mirror and tell each other what we see

underneath the chic posturing seduction, watermelons smashed across the lawn

just for attention, answers to old test questions no longer tucked into our sleeves

i bought that skirt at 16, a nervous virgin at salvation army, and look how

far it's come to crumple in your bedsheets, to kneel down in the parking garage

detergent-stained, top button missing, and kiss the ground like something's

sacred, but it isn't, and then it is, and then it isn't, and then it is

like a searchlight with no target but to spin

disarmed to death

even the absence of ambush is a violent ghost
the air fills with insects wherever caretakers once stepped

in an empty basement, like a frantic chemist
i build a replacement, metallic, out-sprocketed

ill-equipped to insist on gentleness
but would i want it any different?

bless me, hammer of punitive justice
i am addicted to granting permission

for the unspeakable, hand over my mouth
damp impeccable silk sunburnt drunk coming

we say *love* like there is a point to it, but there isn't
just abandoned beaches with all the sharks' teeth

plucked out in advance, every day is a walking talking
divorceable offense, but we're here for it, tantric unflinching

restraints and goggles ready, arriving every moment
disarmed to death, we still see the world end

when we close our eyes
i don't think it will ever stop ending

i don't think it ever has

the solipsist reaches out

i write in search of any ending that lands me a decipherable story

otherwise, where the hell are we? tell me, daddy

but you can't—resurrection comes in percussive waves like

watchdogs under a full moon, swindling grief off its ledges

back into the living—how irresponsible, to decommission

the tin-can telephone's infrastructure

no one could hear us, but we didn't care

the echoes of our own voices were our friends, and we fell asleep that way

deep in the solipsis where nothing was missing

except the sand dunes and fake nails and parking lots beyond help

and the time you almost slit my throat

and the time i almost prayed

impossible gods

i rest my aspirated head on the knees of what is coming
the drive will take all night and by the morning we'll be
nowhere different. the buildings keep busy by measuring
the usual teaspoons of suffering: avalanches over both eyelids
splatter of plasma in the mouth like anything matters
i only get dolled up these days for dates with B52s
blowing the national treasury on a show of proletariat
solidarity over my apartment and we almost miss it entirely
but i catch a glimpse between the rooftops and the treeline
long enough to think, *propulsion's not what i was promised*
the bottles pile up, hard to believe the bad habits, bitter scope
miscarried inheritance lifting into the air like the horseman
of pestilence, the trumpets keep sounding, the seals are all
broken, the revelations of hard drugs are here to save us
from the human race if only we'll take them, i'm ready
to hack the hellscape, levitate into the laughing gas
return a cyborg, i'm ready for the bible to end nothing
like we expected, in the tantrum of a circuit breaker
while we're talking too excitedly to hear
what possible god is brave enough to come near?

Acknowledgments

Thank you to Caitlin Simmons, Christopher Payne, Patrick Gibbens, Andrew Toups, and Garrett Gilpin for inspiring or reading early drafts of these poems. I'd also like to thank the editors of the following publications, where several of these works first appeared:

"belief in evil," "the hierophant hosts a dinner party," and "the rest of history" AKA "exhibitionist's nocturne" (*The Celestial Bandit,* Kernpunkt Press 2021)

"beta haze," "erotics of the soapbox," "give up like you mean it," "minutia trenches," and "very whatever" (*DUETDUET 8*, Pitymilk Press 2023)

"gap in the static," "hallowed be the whores," and "songs i know" (*Unlikely Stories*, 2023)

"the joke," "vetting the ether," "the art of fact," "citizens of what," "the black-box records our defanging," "vcr's last words," "what can perish," and "fossil of desire" (*Not Ready for River Styx: Voices from the Literary Underground*, Back of the Class Press 2023)

"lay-off lilies" and "hail mary, no one is daddy" (*The Holy Hour: An Anthology of Sex Work, Magic, and the Divine,* Working Girls Press 2024)

"textbook anomaly" and "monsters like me" (*Meow Meow Pow Pow*, 2023)

Author Bio:

Dylan Krieger is a child of the Great Lakes and a grownup of the Gulf Coast. She earned her BA in English & Philosophy at the University of Notre Dame and her MFA in creative writing at Louisiana State University. In addition to *No One Is Daddy* (Saturnalia, 2026), she is the author of *Giving Godhead* (Delete, 2017), *Dreamland Trash* (Saint Julian, 2018), *No Ledge Left to Love* (Ping Pong, 2018), *The Mother Wart* (Vegetarian Alcoholic, 2019), *Metamortuary* (Nine Mile, 2020), *Soft-Focus Slaughterhouse* (11:11, 2021), *Hideous Compass* (Underground Books, 2022) and *Predators Welcome* (Limit Zero, 2024). She also serves as managing editor of newsprint literary magazine Fine Print and co-creator of the astrological poem generator at Orb.Church. Find her at dylankrieger.com.

Also by Dylan Krieger

Giving Godhead

dreamland trash

No Ledge Left to Love

The Mother Wart

Metamortuary

Soft-Focus Slaughterhouse

Predators Welcome

No One Is Daddy was printed in Adobe Garamond Pro
www.saturnaliabooks.org